GET INTO CARTOONING

GET-INTO-IT GUIDES

VIC KOVACS

CRABTREE
Publishing Company
www.crabtreebooks.com

Author: Vic Kovacs

Editors:
Marcia Abramson, Philip Gebhardt, Janine Deschenes

Photo research: Melissa McClellan

Editorial director: Kathy Middleton

Proofreader: Wendy Scavuzzo

Cover/Interior Design:
T.J. Choleva

**Production coordinator and
  Prepress technician:** Samara Parent

Print coordinator: Katherine Berti

Consultant: Ramón K Pérez, Cartoonist

Developed and produced for Crabtree Publishing
by BlueApple*Works* Inc.

Photographs

Shutterstock.com: © pistolseven (p. 5 top); © domnitsky (p. 7 left); © Fotana
(p. 7 middle); © cabania (p. 7 right0; © Austen Photogrpahy (p. 6); © Nattika (p.
14 bottom left); © Maks Narodenko (p. 14 right); © Mykola Komarovskyy (p. 22
bottom left);© William Moss (p. 22 middle); © Karramba Production
(p. 22 bottom right)

Illustrations

© Simon Streatfeild cover inset top left, left bottom, top right, back cover, TOC,
p. 8, 9, 10, 11, 12, 13, 14, 15, 16, 17, 18, 19, 20, 21, 22, 23, 24, 25 ,26 ,27, 29, 30, 31
Shutterstock.com: © Kues (cover girl); Denis Cristo (cover boy, p. 4); ©
GraphicsRF (cover -background faces/eyes); © Fourleaflover (wow); © MSSA
(clouds);© Memo Angeles (cover middle left inset, title page, p. 4 bottom left,
11 bottom right,16 right, 17 top right, 22 top right, 23 top right, 24 bottom); ©
Nyuuness (p. 5 bottom); © rudall30 (p. 28); © ATOMix (p. 29 bottom left, cover
middle inset);

Public Domain: James Gillray (p. 4 right)

Library and Archives Canada Cataloguing in Publication

Kovacs, Vic, author
      Get into cartooning / Vic Kovacs.

(Get-into-it guides)
Includes index.
Issued in print and electronic formats.
ISBN 978-0-7787-2638-8 (hardback).--ISBN 978-0-7787-2644-9
(paperback).--ISBN 978-1-4271-1789-2 (html)

      1. Cartooning--Juvenile literature. I. Title.

NC1320.K68 2016   j741.5'1   C2016-903385-6
                                            C2016-903386-4

Library of Congress Cataloging-in-Publication Data

Names: Kovacs, Vic, author.
Title: Get into cartooning / Vic Kovacs.
Description: New York : Crabtree Publishing Company, 2016. | Series:
  Get-into-it guides | Includes index.
Identifiers: LCCN 2016026906 (print) | LCCN 2016027294 (ebook) | ISBN
  9780778726388 (reinforced library binding : alk. paper) | ISBN
  9780778726449 (pbk. : alk. paper) | ISBN 9781427117892 (Electronic HTML)
Subjects: LCSH: Cartooning--Technique--Juvenile literature.
Classification: LCC NC1320 .K68 2016 (print) | LCC NC1320 (ebook) | DDC
  741.5/1--dc23
LC record available at https://lccn.loc.gov/2016026906

Crabtree Publishing Company
www.crabtreebooks.com   1-800-387-7650

Printed in Canada/072016/EF20160630

Published in Canada
Crabtree Publishing
616 Welland Ave.
St. Catharines, Ontario
L2M 5V6

Published in the United States
Crabtree Publishing
PMB 59051
350 Fifth Avenue, 59th Floor
New York, New York 10118

Published in the United Kingdom
Crabtree Publishing
Maritime House
Basin Road North, Hove
BN41 1WR

Published in Australia
Crabtree Publishing
3 Charles Street
Coburg North
VIC, 3058

CONTENTS

CARTOONS THROUGHOUT TIME

The history of what we now call cartoons first began in Italy in the 1700s. This early version of cartooning was called *caricatura*, meaning caricature. It was less realistic than other styles of art of the time, and exaggerated certain features of its subjects to poke fun at them. As cartoons evolved throughout the centuries, they remained unrealistic and mostly humorous. This style is still associated with newspapers. **Political cartoons**, single-panel cartoons, and multi-panel comic strips reach millions of people every day through daily papers.

> What is this?! An F on your math test again?

> Yes, the teacher said that 2+2 still equals 4, regardless of my personal opinion on this matter!

Cartoons have fun with big and small events. Emperor Napoleon (top) carves up Europe in a cartoon from the 1800s, while a modern kid (bottom) flunks math – again.

COMPUTER DRAWING

Today, with the decline of newspapers, many popular cartoons are **webcomics**. Webcomics first appeared at the end of the 20th century. Many of them are about specific subjects, such as science or video games, and have entire websites created around them. Many artists still used the **traditional** methods of pencil, pen, and paper to draw their cartoons. However, as technology has evolved, methods of

Many artists are switching over to fully digital drawing, using state-of-the-art image editing software.

drawing using a computer have become common. Today, digital artists will typically use a tablet and special drawing pen along with specialty software. These tools allow them to digitally create a number of effects that would be more difficult to do with just ink and paper.

CARTOON STYLES

There are as many different cartooning styles as there are cartoonists. Artists need to find the way to best express themselves visually. One particular style that has become very popular recently is manga. This is a Japanese style of comic that includes every **genre** and subject you could imagine. Although there are certain similarities across most manga works, there are still huge variations in style between artists. Only you can create the style that fits you!

Manga developed in Japan after World War II. The stories can be any genre from romance to science fiction.

TOOLS OF THE TRADE

When you're first starting to draw cartoons, it's probably best to use the traditional pencils-and-paper method. An art supply store will have what you need, as well as staff who can make recommendations. Of course, you'll also need something to draw on. A sketchbook is a large, blank book in which you can draw. You will probably need to do some experimenting to find the kind of sketchbook and pencils that work best for you. After you've mastered the basics, you can move up to equipment that will let you draw directly onto a computer.

Different types of paper have different pros and cons. Drawing paper is good for most basic purposes, while something like tracing paper is much lighter and is used to copy examples.

Pens and markers used for inking come in varying thicknesses as well. You can even purchase a whole set to help get you started. For example, the set below is recommended for drawing manga style cartoons.

*You can get a set of art pencils that have varying hardnesses of **graphite**. The harder the graphite, the lighter the mark it leaves. This will let you experiment with different shades and lines.*

Pencils using the HB graphite scale are marked by numbers and letters such as 3B, 4B, or 3H to specify the degree of hardness. The letter "H" stands for a hard graphite pencil. The letter "B" stands for a softer graphite pencil that leaves black lines. For example, a 4B would be softer than a 2B and a 4H harder than an H. Pencils that are marked with "HB" are hard and black. The letter "F" is used to point out that the pencil sharpens to a fine point.

FINISHING TOUCHES

Once you have a finished piece of pencil art, you will want to go over it in pen. This is called inking. Different types of nibs, or pen tips can be used to make thin or thick lines. What you use is often a matter of personal preference. As you learn, you'll also find yourself picking up a variety of erasers. These not only let you get rid of mistakes, but can also help with shading and other techniques. Once you start finalizing your art, you'll also want to look at coloring tools.

WOW!

If you don't have access to a scanner, there are many smartphone apps that allow you to photograph, edit, and upload your art!

Sharp corners on erasers help with defining the edges of your art.

Choose the coloring tools that feel right for you. Try out coloring pens and markers, which are both popular options.

SCANNING

Let's say you've started drawing manually. You've made a super funny cartoon, and you want to share it with your friends online. How can you get it from your page onto your computer? Scan it! A scanner is a device that can capture art, or photos, or any number of other things, and upload them to a computer. If you don't have one at home, your school probably has one. The process depends on the scanner and the computer. With most devices, you lay your art face down on the scanner, close the lid, and press the scan button. It's kind of like a photocopier that copies it directly into a computer. Once you've uploaded the image, you can often use programs to clean it up, color it, or perform other operations.

GIVE YOURSELF A HEAD START

DRAWING FACES

Cartooning is a visual **medium**. A cartoonist can often convey a message by simply using pictures. The most expressive part of a person's body tends to be the face. Knowing how to draw heads and faces should be one of the first things you learn. To begin, draw an oval (or an egg shape). Then draw a cross shape over the oval. This will divide the face into four equal parts. The lines going across the oval will make it easier to position facial features such as eyes, nose, and mouth.

DRAWING HEAD SHAPES

Draw an egg.

Divide the egg with a cross.

Draw three more eggs.

Draw two more small eggs and the letter U!

Erase the cross, color in the small eggs, and add a touch of hair.

Draw two eggs hiding behind for ears, and add some freckles!

Once you have this basic shape, you can begin filling in features. The nice thing about cartooning is your subjects can be as realistic or as simple as you like. Eyes can be just two black dots, or they can be drawn with pupils, colored irises, and more. Mouths and eyebrows can both show a wide range of emotions—even if they're just simple lines. You can also make big, pouty lips and crazy, shaggy eyebrows. A nose can be a simple triangle, or you can give your face full, cavernous nostrils. It's completely up to you.

Eggs are fine, but what about other shapes?

Are the eyes low?

Or are they high?

Have they watched too much TV?

The nose knows.

What does this nose smell?

Small nose!

Big nose!

A simple U will do.

Why not add an M to an O?

Or a P for a tongue?

Remember, a D can make anyone smile!

Eyebrows are essential for emotion.

Are they bushy and bold?

Or slender and surprised?

Eyebrows are simple lines that can add so much!

DRAWING HAIR, EARS, AND MUSTACHES

After you have drawn a basic face, it's time to focus on the outside of the face. What kind of hairstyle does your character have? Is he bald? Does she have long, flowing locks? Whatever it is, you don't have to draw every individual hair. You can draw just the outline of the hair, and that will work. If you wish, you can fill the outline with some simple line marks to provide texture. The same method can be employed with beards and mustaches. Small marks can easily create stubble. You'll also want to give your character a set of ears. One solution is to simply draw C shapes attached to either side of the head, with small Y's drawn inside them. As your skills develop, you can experiment with more realistic looks.

Imagine you are a hair dresser with a magic wand. Fill the hair outline with curls!

Or maybe your character is mostly bald?

Floppy hair hangs down.

Spiky hair does whatever it wants!

The ears here, hear?

Add a Y or two to show the inside of the ears.

Ears can be low C's.

Or high A's!

I mustache you a question!

Can you draw beards and mustaches?

They can be quite bushy.

Or hardly there at all!

GET YOUR CHARACTER IN THE PROPER MOOD!

You do not need overly detailed facial features to show different emotions. Just think of all the different expressions simple emojis can express. It's simply a matter of knowing how to combine the right features to get the look you want. To show happiness, a simple U-shaped smile is enough. Sadness can be shown by flipping that U upside down. Anger can be created with a pair of downturned eyebrows and a slightly downturned mouth. To show surprise, turn your mouth into an O and place the eyebrows high on the forehead. A small mouth and large eyes can show fear or wonder, depending on how you put them together.

Make the expression on your own face first!

Think of something that makes you grumpy!

Or maybe something that is confusing...

Try out different head shapes!

What about an evil egg?

Or a scared square?

Don't be shy! Feel free to overdo the facial features to show how your characters feel.

MIX AND MATCH PROJECT

For this project, start by tracing the head shown in the middle of page 13. Once you have that, try tracing different eyes, eyebrows, noses, mouths, and hairstyles onto it! Experiment to see what kind of expressions different combinations make! You might be surprised at how much a simple pair of eyebrows can change how your character seems to feel. They can go from bored to angry, just like that!

Once you're done combining the facial features, color the faces you created to bring them to life!

SHAPE THE BODY

Now that you know how to draw heads, it's time to put them on top of something! One of the easiest ways to start drawing bodies is to use oval shapes and lines. Once you have the shape and proportion of the body, you can draw more detailed parts over the shapes.

Think about what kind of character you're creating. Is it a big, muscular bruiser? If so, it's probably going to have broad shoulders and large, muscular arms. The shoulders will be much wider than the **torso**. If it's a short, tubby character, the belly will probably be the widest part of its body. Once you have the right body, you can add details. Should you include bulging **biceps**, or maybe frail, twig-like arms? It might help to look at photos or other cartoons to see how bodies are constructed.

Also keep in mind that you will need to draw clothes for your characters. A superhero will probably have a skintight costume, while a business woman would probably be wearing a suit or skirt.

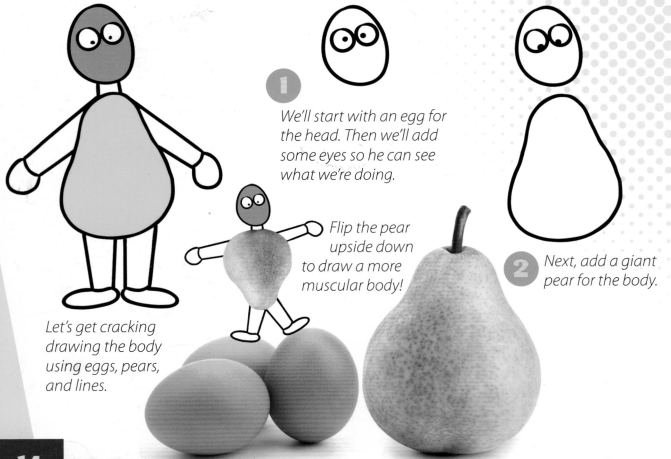

1 We'll start with an egg for the head. Then we'll add some eyes so he can see what we're doing.

Flip the pear upside down to draw a more muscular body!

2 Next, add a giant pear for the body.

Let's get cracking drawing the body using eggs, pears, and lines.

For each arm, we'll add two lines that get slightly thinner toward the wrists!

We can draw some arms at the bottom too...we'll just call them legs.

Better cap off those arms and legs!

We'll add some squashed eggs for his hands and feet.

Better add a neck between his head and body, so his head doesn't float away!

Now you've cooked up a character from your egg, pear, and line omelet!

Color your characters once you're done drawing them.

LET THE BODY DO THE TALKING!

So, you can draw bodies, but what are those bodies doing? Like faces, bodies can be very expressive, even if your character isn't saying anything. This silent mode of communication is called body language. You can convey a lot of information through the proper pose. Think about it. If you come into your classroom and your teacher has arms crossed on her chest, you already know she probably isn't in a good mood.

How happy is your character with his new body?

Maybe he'd be glad to tell you all about it.

Or shocked at his lack of pants!

Perhaps he is upset and disapproving.

Maybe the way he stands shows what he's thinking?

Feeling cool and groovy?

Shocked and startled?

Angry and yelling?

Or bored on the phone?

Maybe she isn't feeling well...

Perhaps he can't decide how he feels.

GET THEM INTO PROPER MOOD PROJECT

Posture often reveals the character's mood. In this project, try tracing the facial expressions from page 18 onto the bodies on page 19. See if you can figure out which face goes best with which body. For example, someone scratching their head would probably have a pretty confused expression on their face, right? An important part of cartooning is figuring out how to have your facial expressions match your body language.

Bright colors will bring your character to life.

Match the facial expressions shown on page 18 and the postures shown above to best fit each character's mood. You may find out that there are several options that will match rather nicely. Turn the book upside-down to find out the matches suggested by the illustrator.

Match 8: H1   Match 7: G2   Match 6: F3   Match 5: E4

Match 4: D5   Match 3: C6   Match 2: B7   Match 1: A8

CREATE THEIR WORLD

Now that you have a character, it's time to figure out where she is! After all, a cartoon of someone standing around in blank, white space would be pretty boring. That said, you don't need to go crazy and draw every little detail. Often in cartooning, simple is better. You would be surprised how a key detail or two can create a complete picture in your reader's mind. For example, if you want to show your character in the mountains, you don't need to draw the entire mountain range and all the trees. Drawing a mountain outline with a few stones and clouds will give the reader the idea. Being able to break down your environment to its basic parts is the key to cartoon backgrounds.

Where is your character? Maybe she's hiking up a giant mountain. First you better give her some ground to stand on.

Then add a wobbly line in the background for the faraway peaks!

Then add some rocks and clouds for detail. Make the clouds smaller toward the horizon and the rocks bigger toward the bottom.

But don't add too much detail! Otherwise the cartoon will be cluttered and you'll lose sight of your character!

PUT IT INTO PERSPECTIVE!

Perspective is a drawing trick that allows you to make a picture drawn on a flat piece of paper look like a 3-D picture. To start experimenting with perspective, try this exercise. First, draw a box. Draw a straight line across the box as shown in the cartoon below. This is the **horizon line**. In the middle of your horizon line, place a dot. This is called the "vanishing point" or the farthest point at which something in your drawing can be seen. Then, draw a V with its point coming from the vanishing point. All lines in the drawing go toward the vanishing point. The closer things are to the reader, the larger they appear. The farther away they are, the smaller they appear. You can play with perspective by moving the location of the vanishing point in your drawing!

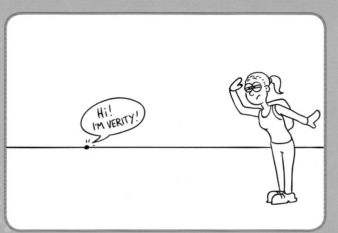

Maybe you want your character to get some perspective! Start with an imaginary horizon line...and pick a "vanishing point." Let's call her Verity the Vanishing Point.

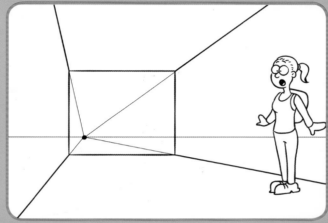

Now we want to create some walls by drawing straight lines that all meet at Verity! You can use a ruler if you want.

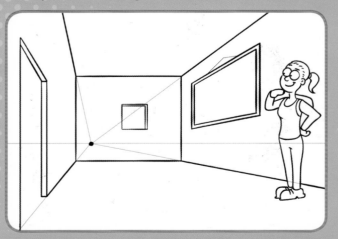

Then we'll add in some doors, windows, and picture frames to brighten up her new home.

Add a splash of color and a rug, and Verity will be proud!

GETTING SERIOUS WITH BEING FUNNY!

So you know how to draw a basic cartoon, but what should it be about? Cartoons can be about anything. Sometimes it can be hard to come up with ideas, but it doesn't need to be! Ideas can come from anywhere! Think about your interests. Do you love dinosaurs? Try making a cartoon about them living in prehistoric times. Do you have a crazy family? Maybe they've been supplying you with material for years without realizing it.

I know it was you who invented the wheel. Fred just says he has some really good ideas for what to do with it.

"Pete's computer wouldn't respond. He suspected the keyboard was broken."

Wooden hotel keyboard and a computer keyboard ... get it?

Make use of words and situations that sound and look the same, and put a little twist on it.

WHAT IS FUNNY?

Humor is an interesting thing. Everyone has different things that make them laugh. Something that will double you over with laughter might not even get a chuckle from someone else. That said, there are a few basics that tend to work well. Slapstick is physical comedy. Think of someone slipping on a banana peel or getting hit in the face with a pie. Some might say that slapstick isn't very sophisticated, but it works! Everyone knows Looney Tunes and The Three Stooges, both of which make heavy use of slapstick.

Why did they lock the watchmaker in a mental hospital? Because he laughed around the clock!

A key element to most comedy is the unexpected. This can come in many forms. The classic structure of a joke is to set up a situation, then **subvert** the reader's expectations with a surprising **punchline**. There are ways to do this both with pictures and with words. Of course, as with the subject of your cartoon, you're the best judge of what's funny. Think about what makes you laugh in real life, and see if you can apply it to your cartoon!

Most people find unexpected things amusing. Try to draw something that breaks people's expectations!

FRED! WHEN I SAID FEED THE CAT... I DIDN'T MEAN TO THE VACUUM CLEANER!

MEOW!

2 HOUR PARKING ONLY

If you're looking to make someone laugh, try to think of something outrageous or unreasonable.

THE POWER OF CAPTIONS PROJECT

Captions are the words that often run underneath the **panel** of your cartoon. They provide the meaning, and make what's going on in the cartoon clearer. They can be a **dialogue** spoken by the characters in the image. They can also take on a narrator's voice and comment on the action in the image. In the cartoons on this page, you can see how changing the caption can completely change what's going on in the cartoon, from the character's motivation to the point of the joke.

"YES, I'LL TAKE THE GARBAGE ENTREE WITH A SIDE TRASH SALAD."

It's important to make sure your caption fits and makes sense!

Just read the latest Food Guide again, it says...less meat and more veggies!

Guys, guys, I thought that we'd agreed on not eating mammoth steaks in front of Hairy Fred. You know it makes him very uncomfortable.

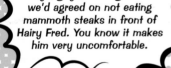

Caption 1   Caption 2

"I'LL HAVE THE SOUP OF THE DAY. PLEASE MAKE SURE THERE ARE NO WAITERS IN IT."

Just by changing the caption on a cartoon, you can change the meaning entirely!

LINES OR BUBBLES?

Captions specifically refer to text outside of the image of your cartoon. If you want to show dialogue within your cartoon, or have two characters speaking to each other, your best bet is to use **word balloons**! These are bubbles that usually have a pointed end facing the character who is speaking. You can also experiment with the shape and look of the balloon to show different emotions. A good rule of thumb is that single-panel cartoons usually have captions, while multi-panel strips usually use word balloons. Of course, there are exceptions to this rule.

1. "FIDO, YOUR HEARING LOSS IS BECOMING A PROBLEM. I SAID 'SLIPPERS!'"

2. "BORIS WAS AFRAID OF HEIGHTS."

3. "YES, I'M HERE TO...VOLUNTEER."

4. "GUYS, I THINK YOU'RE OVERREACTING. I JUST ASKED IF I COULD BORROW $20."

Think of other captions that might fit the cartoons above. Practice the skill of giving cartoons a desired meaning by inventing your own captions to match the scenes. Ask your family and friends for ideas, or take your cartoon to school and ask classmates. Notice how one cartoon scene can bring about different responses from different people, and learn from it. Turn the book upside-down to find out the suggestions by the author and illustrator.

Page 24 – Cavemen: "Guys, there's no point in making a fire if you're still going to eat everything raw!"

Page 25 – 1. "No, Rex, we can't go scuba diving now. You're a dog." "What's this? I don't own a set of flippers. Or a dog?"

2. "Liam the cockatoo was testing out his sense of direction."

3. "I'd like to make a withdrawal." "I would like to open an account, please."

4. "Why are you guys so scared? Is there something behind me?" "Come on, one of you come bowling with me...I have no BODY to go with!"

TELL YOUR STORY

Once you've done a few single-panel cartoons, you can try longer formats. A multi-panel cartoon allows you to do a few things that are impossible in a single panel. The first is showing the advancement of time. Unlike a single panel, which only shows a single moment in time, putting multiple panels beside each other allows you to move forward, and you can show longer conversation. You can also move to another location.

Multi-panel strips come in many formats, but the easiest is the basic three- or four-panel strip. Simply draw boxes next to each other, and fill them in with your characters and a simple joke. From there, you can begin experimenting.

When drawing a comic strip, you want the characters to be consistent.

It's usually good to just show one idea per panel!

Again it's good to break the expectations of your audience...

And finish it off with a funny gag!

FURTHER CHALLENGE – CREATE YOUR OWN COMIC BOOK

If you feel as though you have mastered the basics of multi-panel storytelling, why not try a bigger project? Comic books are one of the most popular cartooning mediums. If you're making one yourself, you have total creative control over it. You could do an entire book of simple, uniform panels, but that would probably look pretty boring. The art of arranging different-sized comic panels is called the "layout." Try experimenting with panels of different sizes and shapes. Some comic book artists are famous for their "splash pages," which are drawings that take up an entire page or two!

When creating a comic book page, make sure you roughly work out where your characters will be located. You wouldn't want any of them to get lost! Fill in the speech bubbles. This will help you work out where things should go.

Next, you want to start using the simple stick figures you made in the first pass. Sketch out what the characters will look like. Then go over the sketches with clean lines ready for coloring!

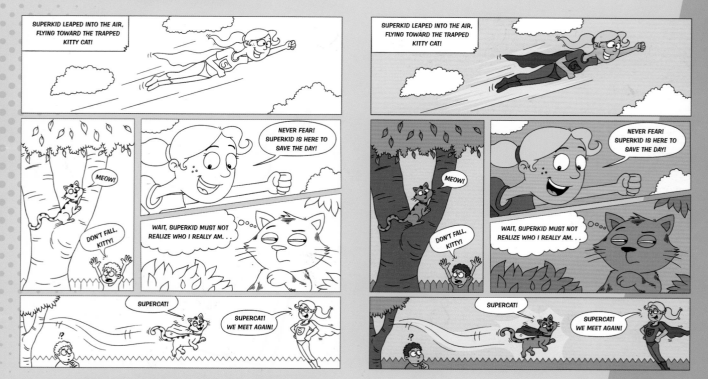

In the next stage, you really want to draw the lines as clearly as possible. Feel free to change things as you go—there's nothing wrong with fixing things along the way. Then we'll start adding in some color...

IS MANGA YOUR STYLE?

Every cartoonist has their own unique style. The only way to find yours is to draw a lot, and figure out what feels right and looks right to you. That said, you can often find inspiration from people who have come before. Find artists whose work you enjoy, and see if you can imitate their style. There's nothing wrong with incorporating elements from your favorites, but make sure you're not just copying them.

Some artists draw more realistically, while others prefer to take a more exaggerated, stylized approach. Both are good options, and only you can decide what works for you. One style that is very popular is manga, or Japanese comics. If you're a fan of Pokemon or Dragon Ball Z, maybe manga is a style you should try! Just like the rest of cartooning, the only real limit is what you can imagine.

Manga usually has young characters at the center of the story, though readers are all ages.

SECRETS OF DRAWING MANGA

Manga characters usually have big, expressive eyes, but their other features are fairly simple. They're also famous for having some pretty crazy hair! There are certain features that most manga share, but there are still as many different styles of manga as there are artists. A lot of manga has heavy slapstick elements, but there are also examples that are very serious. Just like the rest of cartooning, the only real limit is what you can imagine.

WOW!!

Manga specifically refers to comics. Animation in a similar style is called anime!

Manga-style eyes are unique. They are usually big, wide, and full of expression.

Manga characters can be easily recognized by their specific sharp look! They have pointy chins and spiky hair in zigzag patterns.

In manga, bodies tend to have a realistic shape, but you can start with a basic egg for the face and rectangles for the torso.

LEARNING MORE

Books

Cartooning: The Only Cartooning Book You'll Ever Need to Be the Artist You've Always Wanted to Be by Art Roche, Lark Books, 2010.

Funny Cartooning for Kids by Mike Artell, Sterling Children's Books, 2014.

Spectacular Superheroes: Learn to draw more than 20 powerful defenders of the universe! by Dave Garbot, Walter Foster Jr., 2016.

Cartoon Faces: How to Draw Heads, Features & Expressions by Christopher Hart, Drawing with Christoper Hart, 2014.

Websites

The Drawing Website
www.thedrawingwebsite.com
A collection of drawing tutorials for all skill levels.

How to Draw Cartoons Online!
www.how-to-draw-cartoons-online.com
A free site that helps people get into cartooning.

Making Comics
www.makingcomics.com
A site that covers all aspects of creating comics, from drawing to lettering to submitting to publishers.

Manga Tutorials!!
www.mangatutorials.com
A resource that shows how to create manga from the ground up.

GLOSSARY

biceps The muscle on the upper part of the arm, below the shoulder and above the elbow

body proportions The size of parts of the body in relation to each other

dialogue Conversation between characters in a cartoon

genre A specific type of book, movie, or art

graphite The gray/black core of a pencil that leaves marks

horizon line A line that separates the sky from the ground, or divides a drawing into the top and the bottom part

medium The form in which information is conveyed

panel One static image, usually within a single box; cartoons can be composed of one panel, or many strung together

political cartoon A drawing that makes fun of current events and/or politicians

punchline The final line of a joke that usually evokes laughter

subvert Make something weaker or less effective than expected

torso The middle part of the human body, including the chest and stomach; the limbs and neck all attach to the torso

traditional The way things have generally been done in the past

webcomics A cartoon that is distributed exclusively online

word balloon An area in a cartoon in which dialogue is placed

INDEX